ʾNG GRʾSH

ARTIST/POET COLLABORATION SERIES NUMBER TWO

ING GRISH

poems by JOHN YAU

artwork by THOMAS NOZKOWSKI

introduction by BARRY SCHWABSKY

SATURNALIA BOOKS

PHILADELPHIA 2005

Saturnalia Books
13 E. Highland Ave.
2nd Floor
Philadelphia, PA 19118
info @ www.saturnaliabooks.com

ISBN 0-9754990-2-5
ISBN 978-0-9754990-2-3

Book Design by Saturnalia Books

2nd Printing
Printing by Westcan Publishing Group, Canada.

Distributed by:
University Press of New England
www.upne.com
1-800-421-1561

John Yau is grateful to the editors of the following magazines and journals in which many of these poems were first published, often in earlier versions: *American Poetry Review, Brooklyn Rail, Conjunctions, Monkey Puzzle, NO: A Journal of the Arts, Pierogi, The Recluse,* and *Dragonfire.*

Thanks to the Dolphin Press, Maryland Institute College of Art, Baltimore, Maryland, which published an earlier version of English for You. John Yau would especially like to thank Aaron Cohick and Kevin McCabe for the love and care they put into this project.

Acknowledgment is also made to the Foundation for Contemporary Performance Art and the New York Foundation for the Arts for grants that were of immense help to the author during the time the poems in this book were written.

Both author and artist would like to thank Kippy Stroud and the staff at Arcadia Summer Art Program (A.S.A.P.) for all of the help and support they graciously provided in the editing and design of this book.

Thomas Nozkowski thanks Max Protetch and Josie Browne for their generous and continuing support. Stuart Krimko, Chris Davison, James Barber, Amanda Elliott, Peter Harkawik and George Wong of the Protetch Gallery have been invaluable for the creation of this book.

Some of these paintings and drawings have been exhibited at the Max Protetch Gallery (New York), Daniel Weinberg Gallery (Los Angeles), Brett Sikkema Gallery (New York) and the New York Studio School.

ING GRISH

TABLE OF CONTENTS

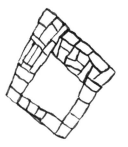

English is well advanced into its inevitable process of becoming pidgin. Inevitable, because when a speaker of English is unaware of the components of words he must speak by formula, rote, and custom, deaf to the historical nuance and blind to the structure of the word.

GUY DAVENPORT

Introduction

FOR ME, IT'S SORT OF A SENTIMENTAL OCCASION—introducing a book when one of its collaborators is John Yau. Ours has been a very long acquaintance, dating back to my very first experience of a "downtown" poetry reading in New York—this must have been some time near the end of the '70s—where he was the reader. We met at a time when he was a new, up-and-coming poet just making his mark and I was something much less than even that. Somehow, though, being a "young poet" never quite suited John. An air of innocence never blew around him. More apropos, somehow, was to be wiser than his years. To be savvy, to be knowing—and to impart what he knew. So by the '80s, at an age when most other poets would still have been scrambling to establish themselves, John was taking an avuncular interest in poets yet younger than himself, giving advice, pointing them toward sympathetic editors, and so on… and I was among those who had the benefit of his support.

It's a funny thing, this desire of John's to create a sort of community around himself—a community of elders and not only of newcomers like myself, for it was thanks to him that I was able to make the acquaintance of heroes like John Ashbery. Because in his poetry, unlike the life he devised to nurture that poetry's conception, he has been a bit standoffish—an isolato. And this despite his eclectic, freewheeling attitude toward formal experimentation, his willingness to learn from and emulate a wide range of poets and poetries, not only contemporary and not only Western. For all that, his poetry has consistently emanated a stubborn, even prickly individualism in its tone, which is quite consistent and, equally, inimitable. Whatever his ties of respect and friendship; the sound of John's verse has never had anything much in common with any branch of the New York School; still less does his poetry have much in common with the Language poets or with any other group or movement one could name. This poetry is too ambivalent to be a good joiner.

In fact, like Groucho Marx who would disdain to join any club that would have the likes of him as a member, this poetry is not even sure it's willing to sign up with the language in which it's written. Syntax and meaning can sometimes come close to falling apart, and for reasons that have nothing to do with any kind of formal exercise in abstraction, chance, or textual autonomy. As the title of John's earlier series "Genghis Chan: Private Eye" suggests, this lexical fracturing has something do with the poet's minority status in American culture. Not that he's ever exactly gone in for identity politics; quite the opposite, his cross-grained stance could probably better be referred to by the yet-to-be defined program that might be called "difference politics". In any case, this private eye has set up his operation under the shingle, ENGLISH BROKEN HERE, and broken it is, from

> *shoo war*
> *torn talk*

through

> *wig maw*
> *mustard tongue*

and on to the very title of the present book. The irony, of course, is that it is precisely because of its passive-aggressive stance toward normative diction that, if the poetry were to answer its own question (in "English for You")—"Do you speak in the American idiom?—then it would have to answer, as indeed it seems to do, "This is what makes me a prime example."

An art critic as well as a poet, John has a long history of collaborations with artists—he's even been known to marry them—but more significantly, unlike other poet/art critics who've taken a more straightforwardly pragmatic attitude toward their seemingly divided loyalties, he's always been determined to get a historical and critical fix on the value of poet-artist collaborations; as long ago as 1984 he edited a special section of *Artforum* on the topic. The fact is, a certain *mestizaje* between poetry and art turns out to be, if you examine the matter closely enough, practically synonymous with modernism—despite, say, Clement Greenberg's diatribes against literariness in art and cheerleading for modernism's supposed tropism toward "purity of medium." Poets and artists are both fascinated with their respective mediums alright—but not necessary out of any concern for purity. They'd just as soon pervert a medium as showcase its chastity.

It was through John, too, that I began to meet artists and get to know the artworld, so it is indirectly thanks to him that, some time in the mid-'80s, I began seeing Thomas Nozkowski's work. Like John, he's one of those figures who is hard to fit in, immune to facile categorization. More than or, perhaps I should say, rather than an influence, Tom has been an abiding inspiration to a good many younger painters in New York and, increasingly, elsewhere. His admirers include more than a few figures of literary note; aside from John, I can immediately think of the poets Marjorie Welish and Ann Lauterbach and the novelist Francine Prose—but he's often been referred to as a "painter's painter." So doesn't that mean dealing with matters entirely "inside" that particular art? And doesn't the fact that his paintings are always untitled suggest that he wants to place them at the furthest possible distance from any literary superimpositions? Up to a point, perhaps. But Tom has also spoken forcefully of "an acceptance and embrace of the peripheral ideas that collect around any art object," and this fascination with the (possible arbitrary and contingent) associations that attach themselves to and modify any perception or memory is at the heart of his working method. If there is a distrust of the word here, it is a misgiving about how the word might limit, might cut off the chain of associations, not a resistance to how language might add to these. What's at stake is a refusal of premature definition.

Each of Tom's paintings—and I was surprised as anyone when I first learned this, for it is far from obvious—begins in the particularity of lived experience, almost as a diaristic observation. "My work is 'abstracted' from reality," Tom said in the same interview from which I've already quoted, "in that each painting has an exact and specific source in the physical world." The originary image, whatever it may have been, gets transmuted through repeated reworking—as a poet might "work" a line by repeating it over and over in his head and letting it transform itself, shift its sound and sense as if he were playing a game of telephone (or as it's sometimes called, Chinese whispers) solitaire—so that eventually it winds up in a form that has been distilled beyond recognition. Matisse, too, spoke of the necessity of transposing one's material as one works it so that the final result might be unrecognizable from its beginning, despite having "a clear vision of the whole right from the beginning."

The results never look like anything but a Thomas Nozkowski painting. And yet, like John, Tom has been open to the widest, wildest range of sources and influences—perhaps because they both have the same confidence that the results will always have integrity. The tone, certainly, of Tom's painting is gentler, more playful than that of John's poems, which are often caustic, but it takes just as fierce a determination to keep them one way as the other. "I have never avoided the influence of others," Matisse, the painter, confided to Apollinaire, the poet. "I would have considered this cowardice and a lack of sincerity toward myself." (Matisse's phrase, "the influence of others," is perhaps translated by the final lines of John's book *Borrowed Love Poems*, 2002: "the claw marks of those / who preceded us across this burning floor".) The point, as both John and Tom know, is neither to assert the self, which would be redundant, nor to escape it, which is impossible, but to question it, to find out what it is made of—and at minimum, to be "able to tell others / that I am not who they think I am." There are a number of idioms in which it is possible to refuse to be identified; poetry and painting are just two of them.

BARRY SCHWABSKY
London

Quotations by Thomas Nozkowski are taken from Sherman Sam's interview of him in Kultureflash no. 67. Henri Matisse is cited from Jack Flam's Matisse on Art, (Berkeley: University of California Press, 1995).

Standard Preface

On a crude woodcut of a heavily laden wagon
Pulled through the air by a string of grinning demons

On a neighbor's sneeze invading the depicted scene
On strange representations buried in secret treatises

On a necklace embracing rainbows and settlements
On this ladder leaning against heaven's deckled edge

On a chair placed before a burning lion
On the morning when fires become more argumentative

On feeding the correct books to riverbeds and tornadoes
On this landscape where shadows have never appeared

On tracing a face encased in a pyramid caked with salt
On overturning a tripod and its four legged attendants

On incredulity, misfortune and enthusiasm
On discarding gods, contrivances, and transparent methods

On sand where writing is completed by prosthetic limbs
On a caterpillar coming unstuck outside the gates of paradise

Even Now

I cannot express the many
sylvan empires of gratitude
I contain, nor adequately
thank you all enough
but I hope that even after I offer
these last few words
these lamentable surrogates,
these inadequate representations,
these roofless domiciles,
that you will still find it possible
to pardon me, who is after all
just a sack of small potatoes,
for not instantly sitting down
with the others made of stone,
but isn't it time to mention
that the dust-filled manuals
that are a true sign of our steadfast frugality
should serve as sufficient warning
to the vast sea of identical vagrants
threatening to turn our charming way of life
into a churning tapestry
others can pick through,
squandering whatever inflamed kernels
they might sift from the unraveling sand,
knowing full well their chances at winning the lottery
diminishes with each new breath.
Might not someone among us
one day many detours hence
choose to pause and remember
that for many carefully annotated chapters now,
we have prevailed against
each caucus of newly arrived waves
because, as uninvited dinner guests,

our lantern-jawed ancestors,
however pitiable they might appear to us
from this end of the telescope,
were able to annex
an untamed vestibule of rapid growth
and mounting interest rates without
becoming vacillating vassals
or, in more familiar parlance,
lowbrow weasels who count
their roman numerals
~~but not their intact crustaceans.~~
True, the wind has a new objective now.
And the movie version has faded
into star-pierced wallpaper
but what flashlight of propaganda
did you believe would succeed
when you left the kennels open,
and let dinner be served late
to packs of rogue ogres
who have remained disappointed
over the reapportionment plan
each lot neat as a tie rack
in a mortician's closet,
as mandated by the sacred vegetables
we consult during sanctioned emergencies,
such as the one that befell the outer compost heaps
during our infatuation with pointed structures.
What exactly marked the first swirling
exit that remembered us? And what
will our whistling do now?
Isn't it time that we revisit
the dribbling string of beads
that leaves us exposed to the cement sky
rumbling toward this moment?

No pageant, no matter how well-planned,
can steep us in the minutiae necessary
to press across the tundra,
but soon we will be ensconced
in our government-issue kayaks and straw kilts,
foolhardy as snakes entering a volcano.
Although much has to be done,
we should remain undaunted
by the distractions dawn dumps outside the dump,
and the train conductors begin saluting
the shadows they think are our president
who is busy petting his stolen dog.
Such is the burden and joy of our legacy
that we should not let it slip into a lobby,
while those of us who can still choke
on our bread and wine and nuts
have yet to do so.

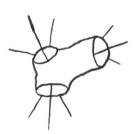

In The Words of Sax Rohmer

A cultured thumb
Varnished and repellant

Of the and with the
Of it and with it

A delicately unforgettable softness
A pointed square

Was it with
~~Was it unforgettable and pointed~~

Yet was it delicately and repellant
Yet was it jointed and long

A tigress with a pointed and slender paw
A possessing hand

A domination cruel
For all its indolence

An unforgettable indolence
Possessing the delicious

A nail's pointed paw
A slender domination

The repellant nails of a cultured tigress
The delicious nails of a long domination

The square nails of an unforgettable hand
The delicately repellant thumb

Of a nurtured indolence
Of a delicious possessing

The cruel and pointed softness
The repellant and varnished softness

The slender and possessing
For all its as and the

A square possessing
The jointed and unforgettable

For all its delicious softness
Cruel and repellant

Of indolence with varnished nails
Of a jointed softness

Of a delicately and possessing
Of a nurtured and repellant

Of an unforgettable velvet square
Slender and long

Screen Name

John Yau is calling, his name has come up on the screen of my cell phone. This makes me uneasy because I am John Yau, and I would like to believe that I am always answering to myself. I decide not to press the green button and see if the caller will leave a message. Since he has my name, and I his, maybe he knows what I was thinking when the phone started vibrating in my shirt pocket, pressed up hard against my nipple, my hands thrust in my pockets, and the air tingling. The shaking subsides, but no envelope indicating that I have received a message floats toward me. I fold up the phone and put it back in my breast pocket. It is Wednesday, and the long-necked geese have started returning to the chimneys of my hometown.

After I realized that I must be the only one who thinks of a cell phone as a cell phone, and not as an efficient means of achieving a heightened spiritual state, I wondered how many friends would tell me the true purposes to which they put their cell phone, and if any found it to be an efficient instrument of physical satisfaction. I decided to call my friends and ask them if they have used or know of anyone who has used a cell phone as a vibrator.

Since the advent of the electric toothbrush, the idea that a common household object could be used to achieve sexual satisfaction of at least the second rank is not a completely foreign particle entering imagination's petrie dish. This hard oblong shape, some with extensions, could have been used in a variety of other ways, but I want to limit the scope of my research. There could be a new definition of phone sex that hasn't become part of our patois.

Might not the following scenario have already transpired countless times in places like Pompeii, Illinois, and Gutenberg, Kansas?? Sheila has gotten out of the shower and, after vigorously drying herself off with her new deep pile purple towel, placed her red cell phone in the appropriate position. After punching a series of buttons, she leans back in her Mies Van Der Rohe recliner, and waits for her favorite daytime romance to come on, a show that is broadcast from an island and therefore not subject to the same restrictions governing similar shows broadcast from places closer to her modest tract home. It is a little past nine in the morning, and Sheila is waiting for her boyfriend Tyson to call, as he does every morning whenever he is away on business.

Standing at a different latitude and longitude is Tyson, who has just jammed his cell phone deep into his pants' pocket. It is Thursday and he is waiting for Sheila to call him, as she does every Thursday that he is away. He is alone at the bus stop, trying to remember which bus will carry him to his destination. He is unsure if he should go north, towards the industrial park, its tasteful array of gleaming towers, or south towards the new amusement center, its computer managed drums of centrifugal force. The sun seems brighter than yesterday, when he was closer to the equator. His phone begins vibrating, slowly at first, and then faster and faster and faster. He is no longer sure what conditions prevail in the time zone that he has entered. Suppose it is Thursday only here, and it is not Sheila who is calling, but his brother who will ask him for a non-refundable loan, or someone from work, checking to see if he has his papers in order. He is glad that he got his and Sheila's phone customized. He was happy to have commissioned a friend of a friend whose specialty is ermine cell phone pouches. His phone keeps becoming agitated, as if its mission remains unaccomplished. Doesn't he have an appointment to meet someone? Isn't he supposed to meet a man by the name of John How or Chow? He is unsure of how to pronounce the man's surname, which sounds simple but a competitive co-worker or jealous underling might have set a trap. Even though it is past noon, he decides he must call Sheila, who has had more experience with the pitfalls one encounters when dealing with foreign names.

A cell phone in another time zone begins vibrating and vibrating. A hand moves it to another location.

Two Baboons on a Beach

It is difficult to adopt the East wind,
and the tan sun cannot be inserted
into the clogged coin slot that one learns
to approach with head bowed.
The laundromat is empty,
its scuffed floors covered
with unidentifiable remnants.
A large black dog is blocking the nursery.
made of basalt blocks,
A demonic dog-like creature
guards the false entrance.
in the culvert behind
a row of precisely painted trees
and climbing flowers.
The demons cavort beneath
a sky of reddish-gold.
Except for a single bathing suit,
the beach is desolate and calm.
Like indulging hemorrhoids in a hurricane,
some states are not easily communicated
when both parties do not share the same tongue.
A boy tells his mother he wants to glue the sky
to the roof of a nearby apartment house.
So, despite a raft of stormy invocations,
the trail of the story grows colder
with each passing hour. The frog
happily hops back into the princess' mouth,
the axe remains indifferent to the pain it causes.
And the last genie decides to retire from active service.
The factory is still humming,
as the hill dissolves in gray mist.
A schoolgirl in a gray and yellow uniform
informs her brother that it would be better

if he pretended that he was a rabbit.
The good Samaritan heaved
the last sack of cold ashes onto the truck,
and then clambered into its dusty cab.
Pistachio ice cream dribbles down
the front of her chartreuse blouse.
A gaggle of troubadors decide to drive to the coast.
The two spinsters living behind City Hall
like to serve different variations of dandelion wine.
Because of the recent rise in petty crime,
the smaller birds nesting near the parking lot
do not fly after dusk, and a young woman eats dinner
alone, by candlelight. The coffee is crimson and warm,
like the sunset flooding the interior of a tower.
Is going into a debt that can never be repayed
the only encore society recognizes
as legitimate? With increasing ferocity,
the bull circles the outhouse marked OFF LIMITS.
The guard gasps when he realizes the owl is missing
but children are rarely if ever old-fashioned, like the clothes
they wear to school during sustained outbursts of freezing rain.
A dog learns to imitate a cow caught in a bear trap,
A bronze-colored man is changed to copper in the town square,
and the ceremony is debated in the local news.
A tall ruddy translator twists the ends of his moustache
according to his inner rhythms, while the president of
a small company desperately tries to obtain opera tickets
for his wife and her two nearly deaf cousins.
Pebbles clatter down a tin roof blazing in the sun.
A servant dutifully burns his master's stables.
A taxi driver follows a school of landlocked fish
being transported to another lake high in the mountains.
No one visits the birdhouse the old man built last fall.

The ants make their way toward a highrise of crumbs,
But other forces will prevent them from reaching their destination,
and this chapter will soon be forgotten by the few still in attendance.
Two silhouettes begin singing a mournful tune
without knowing where it will go. She decides
she wants to own a wind instrument
whose glow has been a source of commentary.
A policeman dreams he is the only policeman in a small town
whose citizens look like they mean business.
The hog decides it is time to let the other animals
~~know that he has carefully charted their future,~~
and this time around it isn't going to be particularly pleasant.
A gust of wind pushes the bubbles into a tunnel.
What are we to do with this last piece of information?
the game show host asked the remaining contestants.
Who has seen themselves running into the wilderness?
Who has studied their sentiments as if their
ingredients had been properly labeled?
Feeling barren, the duke decides to open a chain of cigar stores
named after famous tightrope walkers.
The train reaches the station just before dawn.
Beneath a green sky tinged with pink streams
the Orinoco twists across a thick and muddy plain.
And black clouds roll over the remaining skyscrapers.

Biography for Birds

Lipstick-smeared clouds wrapped in rain
Dormant devotion leaving its destination

I was conceived in the belly of a motorcar
Driven out of heaven by swift angels

My mother stored her clothes in a guitar
Where cows slept beneath yellow apple trees

There was a wagon covered with farms
Sinking into a thick wooden sky

A forked tongue of soot brought more news
From black rectangles chewing in silence

There was a coffin gilded in a silk tunic
There was a bell crammed with warm eggs

I was born at the threshold of golden seaweed
Entangled in memories of a drowned face

Toads restored the ceiling of translucent oxen
Blooming in the middle of a white portico

Successive waves of umber grunts
Lovely without melody or kneeling hisses

I was not the worst of the petals
Battered down by spring's melting kisses

There was an alarm for bedlam clutching
A photograph packed with trickles and salvage

Amber interior ember lips overhead gap
I was born without an introduction

Near the state bakery laments emigrate
Ciphers cruise sheetrock slogs whiskey

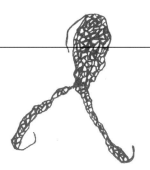

Biography for Amphibians

Harnessed moon enchanting nostalgic armadillos
Clipped tongue erased ornaments flooded sky

Immobile rhizomes sheathed in herbaceous ferment
I am a prisoner of a never released table of contents

The sky is a tin cup sending signals to its children
A cellophane candle sifting through stammering husks

The real voltage is still hiding behind the illustrator's eyes
According to the uniformed woman at the passport bureau

I was probably born yesterday
shortly after a warthog managed to drop me

beneath the effigy of a photograph
I am sitting on a book of codices and partly drawn curtains

Recently most of my limbs have had to be recalibrated
I was invented in the mouth of a receding phantom

Which is why my hair is the color of an extinct wish
According to the alpine clock mounted on City Hall

That crayon dunce cap decorated with crepe paper bells
A secondary character is evincing sympathy

While I am trying to extract the logic of my name
from embers deposited in the fur of this festive prose

I am not sure when I first lost my plural
in the housing projects of the future perfect

Or when I began looking up
the pastimes of my ancestors

Didn't you once threaten to name me
after the ditch beneath your leaded windows

Unpromising Poem

I am writing to you from the bedroom of my ex-wife, where I have been stenciling diagrams on sheets and ceiling, intricate star charts of the paths modern soldier ants take to reach the lips waiting at the end of their long journey. There are no red messages in the balloons floating overhead, no tasty tidbits left from the first meeting. I have been told that the soft meat gets softer in the harsh helixes of the second sun.

I am writing to you from the bedroom of my ex-wife, the room in which flocks of birds have returned to the shelves of their one-syllable caves.
Dust settles on the eyelids of those who have yet to emerge from the shadows. Blue sparks etch the edges where the sky falls away, and black clouds fill the chalkboard with sleeping children.

I am writing to you from the bedroom my ex-wife keeps in her bedroom, the Library of Unusual Exceptions, Book of Gaudy Exemptions, Ledger of Lost Opportunities, wavelengths of archaeological soot drifting through the screen.

I am writing to you from the sleeping car temporarily disabled in the bedroom of my ex-wife. Dear Corraded Clouds, Dear Correspondence Principle, Dear Axle, Enzyme, and Ash, Dear Example of Excellence,
are you Frigg or Freya? Hoop Snake or Hoosegow?

O turtle in a kirtle, why must you chortle so?

Dear Hangman of Harbin, why did I wake in the bedroom of my ex-wife?

Dear ex-wife, I have learned to accept the small pleasures that come with being called The Hangman of Harbin.

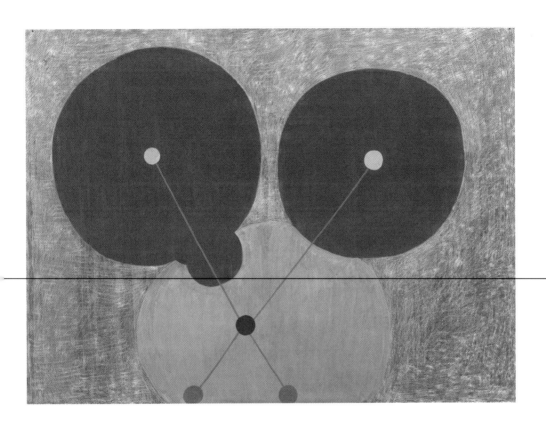

Notes from the Night Editor

A corrupt newspaper publisher takes up painting

Because he wants to depict the nightmarish results

Of his wife's most recent indiscretions

A fake spiritualist swindles a fiend out of his identity

Which a successful doctor finds floating in a pungent liquid

An oracular amnesiac accused of murder

Searches for a missing body with the aid of a con man

Who impersonates the long-lost son of a wealthy couple.

He lives in a cataleptic trance until the embalmer

Waters his prize orchids with formaldehyde

A jealous restaurant proprietor hires

A reformed-gangster's sultry wife

To murder his upscale suburban rival

To gain the confidence of his mentally disturbed secretary

The ghost of a murdered stripper seeks to escape

Her tragic past by taking up residence in a carnival tent

Full of stolen merchandise and gruesome religious symbols

The tailor made her arms look longer by shortening her sleeves

A skeleton covered with blue band-aids pleads

For treatment at a rest stop known for its bat population

A government agent monitors the activity of lab assistants

Who show a preference for red underwear

She collects pillories, guillotines and iron maidens

The horses are agitated by remote control

Rain fills the locked draws of the prison staff

He still likes to listen to crickets in the bathrooms of empty stadiums

A doctor returns to the underground room

Where he keeps the bodies of pyromaniacs

Only to find that two of them are missing

A lion tamer hypnotizes the co-author of a radio play

About a photograph of a wrestling promoter's clairvoyant wife

A pack of poisoned rats sneaks out of a London bank vault

A police lieutenant can no longer report the torment he witnesses

He becomes an ape and starts a ruckus

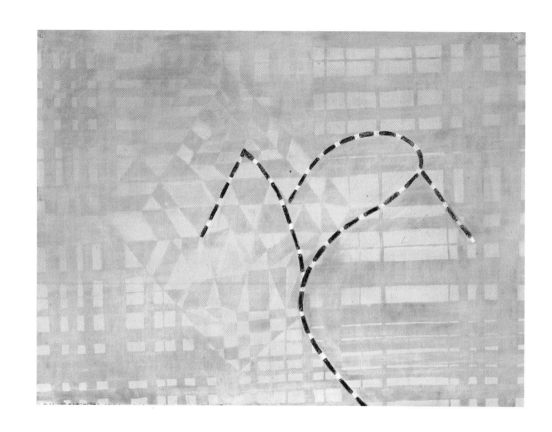

AFTER A CHILDREN'S STORY

Does this mean I am Sam
cave of cold craving
carved and eminently unemployable
destroyer of herds in glasses
mocassins and corduroy
For though thy dreams
be crowded with shiny stanchions
all manner of intelligent rocks
have gathered on dusty shelves of air
but I am no more intelligent because of them
Yes, I am pleased to unseat you
Old Sam of Siam,
inventor of shampoos
for those whose globes
advance like lanterns of warfare
smiter of silhouettes and allotments
For I am Scholar Sam,
king of ducks and ducking out
an infinitesimal particle
considered too small to be an event
And I am youthful Sam,
snoopy stick decked
in iridescent dung beetle
or Sam of Cheyenne
here to discharge
the basis of emotions
battened down by
concentric crescendos
fluttering illusions
guaranteed to shame
and delight
my human crate
wedged in webbing
filled with artificial twilight

Review of the Author

Lack of consanguinity isn't
the only nest egg missing
from this disreputable icebox.
Hindsight's inarguable perfection
also reveals sacks of zero zeal
might have proved a better tuxedo
to have hankered through
clouds of clang and clomp,
their immaculate inundation.
For although he has managed to articulate
a somewhat distinguishable trajectory
from the common colors of the age,
and has refused their demulcent
topsoil of newly arranged nuances,
their recyclable balms for
the boondoggled and bumptious,
but not the borderline and odious,
still he is not sufficiently beholden
to beauty's outsized tongs,
and remains confessedly
out of the circumference of
harmony's rendevous
with anointed swarm of diurnal
slumberers slobbering gracefully
toward epiphanic mementoes,
not to mention that he is decisively
inferior in preparing proper
perspiration of expression,
while also lacking a solid key
to centipede clock of pleasing phrases,
and even ungratefully rejects status
as fully paid member of legendary
legion of lost, missed,

and misunderstood hominids.
Nor is he equal in eloquence
to sediment stirred from
bottom of beaker labeled
Polarized Natural Effects
and subsequently mislabeled
Hallowed Wishes of Wheezing Dipsomaniac
but now thankfully restored to
its proper niche in the porthole
of the varnished moon.
~~More pathetic than tender~~
his soul is not a lantern,
not even a threadbare mufti,
nor defiled mulch in need of
a gust of amatory infusion.
Consider his indelicate sonorities
(a most charitable description)
guilty of barratry,
for his declarations are
embarrassments of wit,
and his style, while not
unintelligible, is a ceremony
from which a heckled
inventory of vanities and vices
fails to yield to indignity's zoo,
heaped by a stack of badly
frocked frauleins who dine on
strings of succulent specimens
made more tender by
their nude effusions of premium stickiness.
His lute has long been superseded
by a starfish's lost limbs
penetrating the dreams of translators

who now speak in another tongue,
having lost their own.
Rightfully accused of being
full of unnatural allusions
while unmindful of
passion's mesquite mortar.
Did he not mistake
his own talents
for that of another?

Guide

On the other side the remnants of a different story than the one you are reading. This flowering scar or scarred tower, this horizon score or implant scare, started when the curtains were parted by a grammar machine presided over by an owl. He is known to possess six facial expressions, none of which help him accrue food on weekends, especially during winter sales. And food is why his cousins, the squirrels, command him to build a table, why three-eyed novelists ponder the procession of phasmids in search of an island dense with vestigial spirals, jubilant and profuse. And then, rather unexpectedly, at least to the audience stirring in their seats, the scientist's store-bought wand turns the chorus into blocks of ice, their serrated mouths exhaling a string of protoplasmic prepositions whose objects, thick with microorganisms, have been misplaced by the Keeper of Fossils and Ferns.

He is not the first prophet to claim that traces of the swamp on which the city was built make themselves evident just before evening exhumes its pillow and moves to the bread factory. An acrid entity begins mingling with the strings of our discarded molecules. Radios emit a fuzzy spreadsheet of unidentifiable numbers. A rumor circulates among the dog walkers that those who live across the ancient highway cut lines into hyena bones, those delightful scavengers of the subways, and that these lines map the few shapes they are still able to safely clutch to their sunken chests. The wind is finally settling into its urn as the rest of us gather on the balcony. The stars are spitting their teeth into the sky.

Alien Documentary

Tomorrow I will
say hello

unpredictable,
agitated

I will walk
upright and smile

hands, tongue,
eyelids quivering

In green air,
under purple sky

I will be elevated
and delirious

My involuntary parts
will not volunteer

"

Untitled Portrait (1)

She is a chanteuse's slender red tiger on her ninth mission. On the planet's leaden floor, four clues protrude from an empty decanter of gamay noir. 1) An Australian weapons master with blue eyes and no tail is stooped over a corpse when an extraterrestrial warrior begins looking at the problem of satellite access for adjunct faculty. 2) An enhanced version from the western belly of the Upper Midlands is aiming her arrow at the second sun from the left. 3) High up in the hills above Booneville, a certified heliotropic breathwork facilitator is being designed and manufactured by the second librarian to receive this rank. 4) She is in the story mainly as a device to work off her criminal charges as part of the Empress's staff of gorgeous opthamologists, all of whom have in their possession a highly coveted glass eye.

Untitled Portrait (2)

An ape is a mechanized program that can be trained to identify a color in a painting as an example of a given. My late husband was also tortoise green, and his hands covered large swatches of imported cloth. I am the orange interruption on the left that still sorts through seeds, trying to determine the life span of their internal combustion. Occasionally an unexpected gust of warmth reaches my uppermost branches. One Saturday a month I squat in a porcelain dome and solicit commentary from those who claim to have fallen through the vast networks of earthbound factions.

A hypocrite is an ape who grips his tongue in all kinds of weather, lest he wishes to court swift and irreversible demotion. Another brand is behind bars and shown at the right, in need of complete restoration. In this corner of the valley, it is not unusual for the ruling ogre to allege that his critics are unlicensed manifestations of the latest technological fads. An ape's only other option is to become fully accredited. The most effective relocated themselves to the neighborhood between horse and rabbit, but have managed to continue dressing in the spirit of a young and stable condition.

Untitled Portrait (3)

You are my forgetful guardian who will not be let back on the team now that you are dead and there are cheaper alternatives. Remember, you are no longer my cat safely sequestered in a paper bag. Yes, it is a mixed blessing to have a large selection of historic artillery pieces on hand, especially when a recent gathering of unpainted pronouns refused to form a manageable circle. Yes, I still live quietly on a one-way street named after the man credited with creating easy access malls. But this has not prevented me from applying for a respectable position in a hotel that caters to travelers planning to contract low levels of amnesia while visiting the Los Angeles vicinity. Yes, he is known primarily as a doctor of unnatural remedies. Last seen detraining in an overgrown hamlet listed in the back of a crime album.

Untitled Portrait (4)

They begin the seventh and final phase of their inquiry into the history of trumpet judgments while listening to the voice of a rubber serpent postpone its latest arrival. One is possibly pregnant; the other is active in the home decorating revival. They have recently suspended their participation in the annual adventure combining remnants of an archaic deception festival with a variety of vehicular reincarnations. Once described in a human interest article as fervent embodiments of contrition. Former claims Pandora is a rising sign, while latter remains mum on this and adjacent subjects. When afflicted with a nervous condition, the taller of the two has been known to say: "A perfect example it is not a theory, it is a mathematical fact." They suspect their neighbors are secretly pondering the aftereffects of circumnavigating their former lives

English For You

1)

I am not going to begin to tell you how
to conduct yourself in this conflagration
but have you ever considered that neither
the clods below nor the clouds above
are getting any younger, and the right
balance of oils, jellies, and powders might be
Just the soporific your cerebral cortex requires
to begin absorbing the sliding calculations
occupying larger and larger portions of the sky
so that there is almost nowhere left
that has not considered any one of us,
And where does that leave us in this landfall
amidst hollows and swellings, layers of smoke
settling softly on the broken ponds

2)

There are words
they want to strip of
their previous function
their identifying faction
how they fit in other mouths
all that has been recorded about them
those who use them and how
with their own mouths
They want to say the words
they are about to be in
the things they say
wanting the impossible
to speak with the same tongue

3)

Will the nearsighted librarian with crooked yellow bangs
translate this article into a streamlined form of English?
Tomorrow, I am expected to distill a new chair for Baby.
Yes, I have already ordered the assistants to type the speech
                                    without correcting it.
Is it simpler than it sounds or simpler than sounds?
When did you ask the waiter to rearrange the tables?
Where is the person who is supposed to bring me my soup?
I demand the bartender bring extra coupons and cartons
                                    just in case.
No one ordered them to start painting the house
Are you suggesting my song belongs in the anniversary issue?
Who convinced the brain surgeon to postpone tomorrow's meeting?
Are you still able to talk freely about your last birthday fiasco?
I asked the cab driver to take me to the hospital,
but he began by refusing to tell me the time.

4)

I cannot repair the rubber scooter all by myself,
but I have to return the washing machine to the store
before the next full moon. I cannot tell the engineers
what is going on inside the rocket, but I have to clean
all the flowers and bicycles before the plumber comes
to look at the ceiling. I am unable to point out a vast
vista of vegetable abundance, but I have to find out
what the typist is doing in the basement. I cannot find
a taxi, but I have to double check and make sure the factory
is delivering a box of bowling balls to tomorrow's convocation.
I ordered another bowl of summer soup ages ago,
but that doesn't mean I know how to use a monkey wrench.
I cannot look up the rest of the words in the dictionary
before I put out the lights, but I can watch you
                              watch your rising inflection.

5)

There is nothing you could do
About what you had done
Once it was another way
A story taking its place in an aisle
But that way was taken apart
You had to do nothing to do
With you it was another you
Who was there in it this time
Who could do nothing once
It was you and you had it all
For there was nothing about
The nothing you could do

6)

There is the man who no longer works at the office.
There is the bus which I have been told had already left.
The man whose position was terminated by mutual agreement
is putting on a coat which doesn't belong to him.
This bus is not the bus I was thinking of when I said
that his job was to put words back into the dictionary.
If he found a word that had previously been lost
or forgotten, he pinned it to the sleeve of a sentence
he slowly filled with sand. He said this was not a metaphor.
He claims words are like artificial planets or plants.
He claims they orbit different suns than the one that warms us.
He claims his office was absorbed by a conglomerate
which believes only unecessary words are missing from the gene pool.

7)

Can I hammer this nail into your article
on agriculture? Did you know the fee
for a pedicure, bath and haircut
for this poodle is more than the day's
take-home pay of an average teacher?
For the first time in the history of the earth
people are able to receive phonecalls
from the moon's surface, where it is a lot greener
than anyone had guessed. Do you remember
the first question to be mistakenly transmitted?
What does it look like from the root cellar of history?

8)

A shampoo and shave is not the same as
taking a public bath, even though they are on
the same street as the Provincial Government.
To take a bath you have to go to a public bathroom,
which is constructed differently than a public toilet.
The best public toilets are tucked away in hotel lobbies.
You can eat in a hotel, even if you don't sleep there,
and you can sleep in a hotel, but you don't have to eat there.
Yesterday they opened a power plant in the green hills.
They also opened many schools where you cannot see them.
Are you an auxilliary predicate or an associate adjective?
Please hang up and wait for the roof to close.
He's a reporter, foreign correspondent, manager of
military telephones. He wears a hat. He's hungry and dirty.

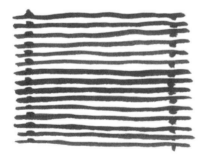

9)

Let's embellish the story about brown shoes and black shoes
and the man who forgot the word for "telephone."
Let's go to the Museum of Unnatural History
and look at books about the mining industry.
Let's call high officials "important people of Party and Country."
Let's take an airplane trip to a small town
where there are no religions and lie
about the party at the Transportation Fair.
Let's name the capitals of rural municipalities
after men and women who have made the prices
go down and still supported their families.
Let's not repeat the story of the man
who was afraid to go to the post office after dark.
Let's admit not a single one was allowed to go home.

10)

Let us say the sky is gray, but all that is gray today
is a woman walking into town with a pink envelope
pressed against her right cheek. Let us say
she is a sophomore in the Military Academy
but she no longer remembers the words of her
high school anthem. Let us say every afternoon
between two and four there is a telescope for rent.
Let us say "barracks," "trenches," "storeroom
for drugs," and "wounded soldiers's amusement club."
Let us say that she has never been to Finland
or seen a picture of a reindeer, a walrus, a rotting keel.
Let us say that it is only by an accident of history
that we tend to call both languages by the same name.
Let us say refrigerated noise has been invented.
Let us say we remember all the I's and you's
who perished in the Great Pronoun Wars of the last century.

11)

You can consult the oracle to learn if separating
is better than branching out, living separately
is more advisable than living under separate
covers or withdrawing into different paragraphs.
You can disentangle, bid farewell, sell off, run out.
The oracle may advise you to search for a notice,
wait to receive a bulletin, demand a revision,
endure cold-heartedness and cold shoulders
The farewell gift will arrive in the form of
a voluminous opinion, an expansive address,
a separate paragraph enclosed in a letter.
The sentence will be a sentence rather than
a judgement, notice of sale, evidence of drainage.
It will complain about an unusual matter

                        in an unusual way.

12)

Are you transmitting your past life
or are you being reintroduced to it?
Blossoms released in a labyrinth.
Skirt or stand, boast of or glory in,
priceless or precious. When the remains
remain an impudent thickness or cheeky density,
a conspicuous element in a chest of drawers
marked "National Policy or Hidden Premise,"
one cannot forfeit posthumous invoices,
testaments or legacies still need to be sprung
or rejected, bribes or trades igniting a shudder
or blackened rustle, perhaps a loss of money
or stolen inheritance, a collapse or stampede,
denunciations to sell in the market, purchased wholesale,

                            overestimated.

13)

Either you eat meat or you hide a wooden fish
in each suitcase before going to the airport.
Either you are seen frequently or you diminish in size.
Either you slip on the ice or you shine
like a substandard loudspeaker at a management rally.
Either you sneeze between gulps
or you squeeze the mud until a wireless radio
orders you to publicly admit all your superstitions.
Either you become moist or you leave in a hurry,
forgetting to steal a book of pornographic letters
from your neighbors, many of whom claim to be sterile.
Either you lie down and lie or you begin to talk
about how this photograph was replaced by air.

14)

Do you speak in the American idiom?

Have you had all your buttons
yanked lately, baby? Why yes,
I am as fluent as a fish in water,
In fact, even when I am lying
relaxed at the bottom of a swimming pool,
I can speak, write, and whistle
in the American idiot you glow on about.
You can tell by my baseball cap.
No team has this logo, which means
it stands for me and is therefore all mine
(in case you are wondering, I designed
it myself, down to every last tooth and nail).
This is what makes me a prime example.
No one is so stupid as to speak or write otherwise.

15)

And all along if they did what we thought
they were going to do if we said what
we were going to do once they did what
they did was that what they were going to do
all along and would we say later that all along
we knew what we were going to do if they and they did
even if they didn't say it and what if what
we said they didn't say was what we said
we heard them say would we tell them
if all they thought was they were going along
with what we said we would do what would they say
we did say what if we say what we thought was once said
wasn't said would we say later that the we was they
and if we did would we later say we didn't say it

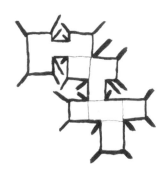

LANGUAGE LESSONS

Once there are too many questions
And then there are not enough

Do you dream in your native tongue
Or is it someone else's tongue
that is waging war

Satisfactory is a grade
as is
Almost not quite good enough

It depends upon your pronunciations
It depends on whether the emphasis
Is on *phlegm* or *ish*
As in
do you speak *Flemish*

On occasion I have been known to speak *Phlegm*
A language that leaves an impression on the listener
When the speaker is insistent or emphatic

Being the recipient of *Phlegm*
Does not mean one understands *Flemish*

Does the narrator in this story
Expect to expectorate
Or is this an
exception
exemption
example

What does it mean to not know
Which half is *Irish*
That the tongue does not speak
Either *Irish* or *You-Ish*
It means the world
is neither crying nor smiling

CORRECT ANSWERS

The fortune teller was beyond reproach
They sent each other sentimental poems
They told stories haunted by their dead selves
They did not bless him when he entered his bed
It was, they told him, a coffin that would eventually fit him
They mourned their childhood whenever
the opportunity arose which was often
He was born with evil leaking from every pore
They told him it was self-inflicted
They were convinced that they never lied or exaggerated
They slept in a trench full of rain
and believed, until the day they died,
that something more terrible was imminent
They laughed when he told them that he was running away

Diaspora

My father shifted in his chair and turned the page. He was reading the diary of a cavalry officer who admired the versatility of his adversaries.

Upside down, the wok looked like a flying saucer, so I carefully surrounded it with rows of plastic Indians and Cuban gueriillas dressed like American marines. The only problem was that none of them had beards. It was the Fifties but already I was on the wrong side.

She seldom told me who was speaking, only that she was being spoken too.

History is fraught with those who failed to heed the music wafting right under their noses. Perhaps we will know where tiome once once we get there.

All day the spaceship sat on the Great Plains of the dining room table my parents carried with them whenever they moved. Rooming house until she saw another tenant pissing in the sink. Basement apartment with steam pipes. Two room storefront with glass bricks between living room and sidewalk. Six floor walkup. First floor apartment. Two family house, the couple who lived in the other half owned the restaurant and a Chinese restaurant a few blocks away. House with garage and backyard on a dead-end street. The American dream is increasing your ability to be in debt. When they finally could afford to owe twenty-thousand dollars, they were proud of what they had accomplished.

Thirty-five years later, the dream nearly over, I cover the table's worn surface with a clean tablecloth, check to make sure there is more than enough food in the refrigerator, and that the beer is getting cold. I walk out to the car and wait to drive my father and brother to the building where she is lying in her coffin, her eyes closed at last. Even though the snow has started to melt, and the icicles above the garage door are dripping, it is a languorous morning.

I want to tell her that they left long ago, and that their mission was fulfilled.

Ing Grish

You need to speak Singlish to express a Singaporean feeling.

CATHERINE LIU

I never learned Singlish

I cannot speak Taglish, but I have registered
the tonal shifts of Dumglish, Bumglish, and Scumglish

I do not know Ing Grish, but I will study it down to its
black and broken bones

I do not know Ing Gwish, but I speak dung and dungaree,
satrap and claptrap

Today I speak barbecue and canoe

Today I speak running dog and yellow dog

I do not know Spin Gloss, but I hear humdrum and humdinger,
bugaboo and jigaboo

I do not know Ang Grish, but I can tell you that my last name
consists of three letters, and that technically all of them are vowels

I do not know Um Glish, but I do know how to eat with two sticks

Oh but I do know English because my father's mother was English
and because my father was born in New York in 1921
and was able to return to America in 1949
and become a citizen

I no speak Chinee, Chanel, or Cheyenne

I do know English because I am able to tell others
that I am not who they think I am

I do not know Chinese because my mother said that I refused to learn it
from the moment I was born, and that my refusal
was one of the greatest sorrows of her life,
the other being the birth of my brother

I do know Chinese because I understood what my mother's friend told her
one Sunday morning, shortly after she sat down for tea:
"I hope you don't that I parked my helicopter on your roof"

Because I do not know Chinese I have been told that means
I am not Chinese by a man who translates from the Spanish.
He said that he had studied Chinese and was therefore closer
to being Chinese than I could ever be. No one publicly disagreed with him,
Which, according to the rules of English, means he is right

I do know English and I know that knowing it means
that I don't always believe it

The fact that I disagree with the man who translates from the Spanish
is further proof that I am not Chinese because all the Chinese
living in America are hardworking and earnest
and would never disagree with someone who is right.
This proves I even know how to behave in English

I do not know English because I got divorced and therefore
I must have misunderstood the vows I made at City Hall

I do know English because the second time I made a marriage vow
I had to repeat it in Hebrew

I do know English because I know what "fortune cookie" means
when it is said of a Chinese woman

The authority on poetry announced that I discovered that I was Chinese
when it was to my advantage to do so

My father was afraid that if I did not speak English properly
I would be condemned to work as a waiter in a Chinese restaurant.
My mother, however, said that this was impossible because
I didn't speak Cantonese, because the only language
waiters in Chinese restaurants know how to speak was Cantonese

I do not know either Cantonese or English, Ang Glish or Ing Grish

Anguish is a language everyone can speak, but no one listens to it

I do know English because my father's mother was Ivy Hillier.
She was born and died in Liverpool, after living in America and China,
and claimed to be a descendants of the Huguenots

I do know English because I misheard my grandmother and thought
she said that I was a descendant of the Argonauts

I do know English because I remember what "Made in Japan" meant
when I was a child

I learn over and over again that I do not know Chinese.
Yesterday a man asked me how to write my last name in Chinese,
because he was sure that I had been mispronouncing it
and that if this was how my father pronounced it,
then the poor man had been wrong all his life

I do not know Chinese even though my parents conversed in it every day.
I do know English because I had to ask the nurses not to put my mother
in a straitjacket, and reassure them that I would be willing to stay with her
until the doctor came the next morning

I do know English because I left the room when the doctor told me
I had no business being there

I do not know Chinese because during the Vietnam War
I was called a gook instead of a chink and realized
that I had managed to change my spots without meaning to

I do not know English because when father said that he would
like to see me dead, I was never sure quite what he meant

I do not know Chinese because I never slept with a woman
whose vagina slanted like my mother's eyes

I do not know either English or Chinese and, because of that,
I did not put a gravestone at the head of my parents' graves
as I felt no language mirrored the ones they spoke.

JOHN YAU is the author of many books of
poetry, fiction, and criticism, including *Borrowed
Love Poems* (2002), *Hawaiian Cowboys* (1995),
and *The United States of Jasper Johns* (1996).
His collaborations with artists have been exhibited
at the Museum of Modern Art (New York),
Bonn Kunstmuseum, Queensland Art Gallery
(Australia), and Centre Pompidou, as well as at
Volume, Ethan Cohen, and Phyllis Kind Gallery.
He has received grants and fellowships from the
Foundation of Contemporary Performance Art,
the New York Foundation for the Arts,
the National Endowments for the Arts,
the Ingram Merrill Foundation, and
the Peter S. Reed Foundation, as well as a
General Electric Award, Lavan Award (Academy
of American Poets), and Brendan Gill Award.
In 2002, France named him a
Chevalier in the Order of Arts and Letters.
He is on the faculty of the Mason Gross School
of the Arts (Rutgers University).

THOMAS NOZKOWSKI is a painter who
has had over sixty one-person shows of his work.
His most recent exhibitions include those at the
Max Protetch Gallery, New York and the
Daniel Weinberg Gallery, Los Angeles.
Survey exhibitions of his work include those at
Haunch of Venison, London (2004), the
New York Studio School (2003) and the
Corcoran Gallery of Art, Washington (1996).
He is represented in the collections of the
Addison Gallery of American Art, the
Brooklyn Museum, the Corcoran Gallery of Art,
the Hirshhorn Museum and Sculpture Garden,
the Metropolitan Museum of Art, the Museum
of Modern Art, the Phillips Collection and the
Whitney Museum of Art among others. He is a
Guggenheim fellow and has received an
American Academy of Arts and Letters Award
in Painting. He is Professor of Painting at the
Mason Gross School of the Arts
at Rutgers University.